Copyright © 2024 by Brian Ernest Hayward and Published by Brian Hayward for Hayward House Publishing Published by Hayward House and Big Book Box A Member of the Brian Hayward Group All rights reserved. No part of this publication may be reproduced, stored in a retrieval system, or transmitted, in any form or by any means, electronic, mechanical, photocopying, recording, or otherwise, without the prior written permission of the publisher. For information and inquiries, address Hayward House publishing and Hayward Press, Savannah, Ga 31405, Library of Congress Cataloging-in-Publication Data. Hayward, Brian. TITLE=In Jesus Mighty Name Series, Journal WRITING for success in your life / Brian Hayward. p. cm.

PAPER BACK EDITION
ISBN: 9798333959423

Imprint:
Independently published

Self-control. 2. Self-management (Psychology) 3. Success. 4. Success in business. 31405, or visit us at https://www.amazon.com/Brian-Ernest-Hayward/e/B06XT464NM

PRAYER FOR MYSELF AND MY READERS

I was taught by my teacher, Pastor Bill Winston, this prayer. This prayer has served me well, and in due time it will serve you well. Father I come before you in Jesus name, thank you for the anointing that's on me and these lips of clay. I know that because of your blessing, I speak this word today with excellency, accuracy, and boldness. I thank you for thinking through my mind and speaking through my lips and this word will come forth unhindered, and unchecked by any outside force. Now I give you the praise for it and I fully expect signs, wonders, and miracles to confirm your word preached in Jesus name,

AUTHOR BIOGRAPHY

Brian Ernest Hayward is a passionate Author and Inspirational Speaker, internationally known for his unwavering dedication to creating positive change through the power of words. From religious and success books, to adult coloring books and artist BUSINESS, HOW-TO BOOKS, his writings touch on over 400 different subjects. Today, all of Brian's publications are sold worldwide across multiple formats (Paperback, Kindle, and Large Print) and are translated into 21 different languages. He has also participated in over 100 speaking engagements spanning over 38 states.

Table Of Contents

Introduction-Lazy Rich: Snooze, Cash In, and Rise When You Want - The Ultimate Auto Pilot Hustle Guide ... 7

Chapter 1: The Allure of Passive Income ... 20

Chapter 2: Finding Passive Income Opportunities ... 20

Chapter 3: Building a Strong Foundation – Financial Planning and Management ... 39

Chapter 4: Creating Automated Online Businesses ... 48

Chapter 5: Investing in Real Estate for Passive Income ... 56

Chapter 6: Using Investments and Dividends ... 66

Chapter 7: Creating and Selling Digital Products ... 74

Chapter 8: Building and Monetizing a Blog or YouTube Channel 82

Chapter 9: Balancing Initial Effort with Current Responsibilities 90

Chapter 10: Conclusion – Embracing the Auto-Pilot Hustle Lifestyle 98

Chapter 11: Nurturing a Growth Mindset for Sustained Success 105

Chapter 12: Giving Back and Creating a Legacy 114

Nap-time Net-worth Neutron Cash Cushion Climax Conclusion 124

Bibliography 141

NOTES 143

Introduction-Lazy Rich: Snooze, Cash In, and Rise When You Want - The Ultimate Auto Pilot Hustle Guide

How to Stay in Bed, Make Money, then Get Up Only When You Feel Like It: The Auto Pilot Hustle Book. Welcome to the revolution in financial freedom and lifestyle design! Imagine waking up without an alarm clock, stretching luxuriously in your cozy bed, and  knowing that while you were enjoying sleep, your bank account was steadily growing.

This is not a fantasy reserved for the ultra-wealthy or tech moguls. This is  the promise of the auto-pilot hustle, a lifestyle where Money flows in effortlessly, and you get up only when you feel like it.

In this book, "How to Stay in Bed, Make Money, then Get Up Only When You Feel Like It: The Auto Pilot Hustle Book," we will embark on a journey to turn this dream into your reality.

Over the next few months, we meticulously crafted this guide, pouring in countless hours of research, real-life experiments, and expert consultations. Month one was all about deep diving into the myriad ways to generate passive income. We explored investments, real estate, online businesses, royalties, and much more, gathering insights from those who have mastered the art of making Money while sleeping. This foundation laid the groundwork for understanding the vast landscape of passive income opportunities available in one month, and we shifted our focus to practical implementation. We broke down complex concepts into actionable steps, tested different strategies, and refined our approach.

Our goal was to ensure that this book not only provides you with knowledge and equips you with the tools to take immediate action. We delved into financial planning, risk management, and time optimization, ensuring you have a robust framework to support your passive income journey.

The final month was dedicated to real-world applications and case studies. We interviewed individuals who have successfully transitioned to the auto-pilot hustle lifestyle, learning from their successes and challenges. Their stories serve as both inspiration and proof that this lifestyle is achievable. We also fine-tuned the book, ensuring every chapter is packed with value, practical advice, and a touch of humor to keep you engaged and motivated.

So, why is this concept needed, and how can it be applied in day-to-day business? The modern world is fast-paced and often overwhelming. Traditional work models demand long hours, leaving little room for personal pursuits, family time, or simply enjoying life. The auto-pilot hustle offers a solution to this predicament. By building multiple streams of passive income, you can free yourself from the constraints of a 9-to-5 job and design a lifestyle that aligns with your values and desires.

The principles of the auto-pilot hustle can be a meaningful change in day-to-day business. Imagine running a company where systems and processes are so well-designed that your involvement is minimal, yet the profits keep rolling in. This book provides strategies to automate your business operations, delegate effectively, and leverage technology to significantly reduce your workload. The goal is to create a busy, thriving business from your constant input, allowing you to focus on high-level strategy, innovation, or simply relaxing.

Let us explore how this book is structured to maximize your learning and application. The chapters are meticulously organized to guide you step-by-step, from understanding passive income fundamentals to implementing advanced strategies. Each chapter builds on the earlier one, ensuring a seamless progression of knowledge. Practical exercises, real-life examples, and case studies are integrated throughout to reinforce learning and inspire action.

Chapter One sets the stage by exploring the allure of passive income. We start with a captivating story highlighting the benefits of a relaxed lifestyle supported by passive income. We define passive income, explain its significance, and provide an overview of the book's roadmap. This chapter is designed to hook and excite you about the possibilities ahead.

In Chapter Two, we dive into finding passive income opportunities. You will learn about various passive income sources, including investments, real estate, online businesses, and royalties. We guide you in assessing which opportunities best suit your skills, interests, and resources. Real-life case studies give concrete examples of individuals who have successfully implemented these strategies.

Chapter Three focuses on building a solid foundation. We cover the basics of budgeting, saving, and investing, emphasizing the importance of financial planning in supporting your passive income ventures. Risk management strategies are discussed in detail, ensuring you are well-prepared to navigate potential pitfalls. Practical tips and exercises help you apply these concepts to your financial situation.

In Chapter Four, we explore the creation of automated online businesses. From e-commerce and drop shipping to affiliate marketing, you will learn how to set up and run businesses that generate income on autopilot. We include a case study of a successful online business, detailing its setup, management, and ongoing operations. This chapter provides actionable steps to get your online business up and running.

Chapter Five delves into real estate investing for passive income. We discuss purchasing, managing, and profiting from rental properties. REITs and crowdfunding platforms are also covered as alternative ways to invest in real estate without direct property management. A real-world example illustrates how an individual can earn passive income through real estate investments.

Chapter Six is all about using investments and dividends. You will learn the basics of investing in dividend-paying stocks and bonds, building a diversified portfolio, and generating passive income through intelligent investment strategies. A case study of a successful investor provides insights into their approach and results.

Chapter Seven focuses on creating and selling digital products. We discuss how to develop and market digital products like eBooks, courses, and software, using platforms like Amazon, Udemy, and Shopify. An example of a successful digital product creator's journey provides practical insights and inspiration.

Chapter Eight explores building and monetizing a blog or YouTube channel. You will learn content creation strategies, monetization methods, and tips  for attracting and keeping an audience. A case study of a blogger or YouTuber who has turned their content into a passive income source provides real-world inspiration.

Chapter Nine addresses balancing initial efforts with current responsibilities. Effective time management strategies, outsourcing, and delegation are discussed in detail, ensuring you can build passive income streams without burning out. Practical tips and exercises help you keep balance and avoid common pitfalls.

Finally, Chapter Ten wraps up by embracing the auto-pilot hustle lifestyle. We recap vital lessons, emphasize the benefits of  passive income, and encourage you to think long-term. An inspiring call to action motivates you to start your journey towards financial independence and a leisurely lifestyle today. A memorable ending with an inspirational story or quote leaves a lasting impact, reinforcing the value of the auto-pilot hustle.

This book gives practical advice, real-life examples, and a touch of humor to keep you engaged and motivated. The journey to financial independence and a relaxed lifestyle is within your reach. This book is your guide to making it happen. So, grab a coffee, settle into your favorite chair, and prepare to transform your financial future with the auto-pilot hustle.

Welcome to the first step of your journey to financial freedom and a life designed on your terms. Let us dive in and explore the incredible possibilities that await you.

Chapter 1: The Allure of Passive Income

There is a universal appeal to making Money while you sleep. Imagine waking up, stretching luxuriously  in your bed, and knowing that while you were dreaming, your bank account was getting a little fuller while you; it was dreaming. This is not while you were dreaming just a fantasy for the ultra-wealthy or the tech-savvy.

With the right mindset and strategies, passive income can be within anyone's reach. It is about using your time and resources to create streams of income that flow in, even when you are not actively working. This chapter will take you on a journey into the captivating world of passive income, a lifestyle that promises financial security and the freedom to spend your time as you please.

Let us start with a story. Picture a young professional exhausted from a 9-to-5 job, barely finding time for family or hobbies. They stumble upon the  concept of passive income and decide to take a leap of faith. Fast send a few years, and this same individual is living comfortably, with multiple income streams providing stability and freedom. They travel, pursue passions, and enjoy life without the constant stress of financial worry. This is not a fairy tale; it is a reality for many who have embraced the passive income lifestyle.

But what exactly is passive income? Simply put, it is Money earned with minimal effort. Unlike active income, where you trade hours for dollars, passive income continues to flow with little to no ongoing work. This can come from investments, rental properties, online businesses, royalties, and more. The key is to set up these income streams properly, requiring some first effort and often some ongoing maintenance, but nothing compared to the continuous effort of a traditional job.

This book is your roadmap to achieving that dream. We will explore various passive income opportunities, from real estate to digital products, and provide practical steps to help you build and keep these income streams. We will dive into real-life examples and case studies to show you what is possible and inspire you to act. Each chapter is designed to build on the last, guiding you through the process of creating a sturdy foundation, finding the right opportunities, and managing your income streams for long-term Success.

As we embark on this journey, it is important to recognize that while passive income can lead to a more relaxed lifestyle, it requires initial dedication and smart planning. This is not a get-rich-quick scheme but a sustainable way to build financial independence. By the end of this book, you will have a clear understanding of passive income, practical strategies to implement, and the motivation to start your journey towards a freer and fulfilling life.

In the coming chapters, we will delve deeper into specific types of passive income. You will learn about the ins and outs of investing in real estate, the potential of digital products, the power of dividend-paying stocks, and the vast opportunities in online businesses. We will also cover essential financial planning and management strategies to ensure your passive income journey is smooth and successful.

One of the most critical aspects of achieving passive income is finding the right balance between first effort and ongoing management. We will provide time management techniques and tips for outsourcing and delegation, helping you keep your current responsibilities while building your passive income streams. The goal is to set up systems that work for you, freeing up your time to enjoy the things that truly matter.

Throughout this book, we will use a friendly, humorous tone to make the information engaging and accessible. We want you to not only learn but enjoy the process. Building a passive income lifestyle should be fun and rewarding. So, sit back, relax, and get ready to transform your financial future.

To give you a sneak peek, here is a brief overview of the chapters ahead. We will start with finding various passive income opportunities and help you assess which ones are best suited for you. Then, we will move on to building a strong financial foundation, covering budgeting, saving, and investing basics. From there, we will dive into specific strategies for creating automated online businesses, investing in real estate, using investments and dividends, and more.

Each chapter will include practical tips, case studies, and step-by-step guides to help you implement what you have learned. By the end of this book, you will have a comprehensive understanding of passive income and the tools to start building your streams. Whether you are looking to supplement or completely replace your current income, this book will offer the guidance you need.

Now, let us get started on this exciting journey. Remember, the path to passive income is not a sprint but a marathon. It requires patience, persistence, and a willingness to learn and adapt. But with the right approach, the rewards can be life changing. So, grab a cup of coffee, settle into your favorite chair, and let us dive into the world of passive income together.

In the following chapters, we will explore the several types of passive income in detail. We will discuss the pros and cons of each, give real-world examples, and offer practical advice on how to get started. Our goal is to equip you with the knowledge and confidence to take control of your financial future.

We will also address shared challenges and pitfalls along the way. Building passive income streams is not always smooth sailing, but you can overcome any obstacles with the right strategies and mindset. We will share insights and lessons from those who have successfully navigated the journey, so you can learn from their experiences and avoid common mistakes.

 By the time you finish this book, you will be well on your way to creating a more flexible and fulfilling lifestyle. You will have the tools and knowledge to build multiple streams of passive income, allowing you to enjoy more freedom and less stress. So, let us embark on this journey together and discover the power of passive income.

Remember, passive income aims to create financial stability and freedom. It is about using your time and resources to build a more secure future. With the right approach, you can achieve your financial goals and enjoy the lifestyle you have always dreamed of. So, let us get started on this exciting adventure and unlock the potential of passive income.

Chapter 2: Finding Passive Income Opportunities

Diving into the world of passive income begins with understanding the variety of opportunities available. One of the most appealing aspects of passive income is its diversity. There's no one-size-fits-all approach, meaning you can tailor your passive income strategy to fit your skills, interests, and resources. This chapter will guide you through the diverse types of passive income, helping you find the best opportunities for your unique situation.

First on the list is real estate. Investing in rental properties has long been a fashionable way to generate passive income. With the right property, you can earn a steady stream of rental income while also receiving help from property appreciation over time. Real estate can provide both short-term cash flow and long-term wealth building, making it a versatile choice for many investors. However, it is important to carefully consider location, property management, and market conditions to maximize your returns.

Another lucrative avenue is the stock market, particularly through dividend-paying stocks. You receive regular dividend payments when you invest in companies that distribute a part of their profits to shareholders. This can provide a reliable income stream without the need for constant trading or market monitoring. By building a diversified portfolio of dividend-paying stocks, you can achieve a balanced mix of growth and income.

Online businesses offer a vast array of passive income opportunities. E-commerce, affiliate marketing, and digital products are just a few examples. E-commerce platforms like Shopify allow you to set up online stores that can run entirely on autopilot. Affiliate marketing involves promoting other people's products and earning a commission on sales, which can be done through blogs, social media, or email marketing. Once created, digital products, such as eBooks, online courses, and software, can generate ongoing revenue with minimal upkeep.

Investing in peer-to-peer lending is another choice to consider. This involves lending Money to individuals or small businesses through online platforms, earning interest on your loans. It can offer higher returns than traditional savings accounts or bonds, but it is essential to understand the risks involved and diversify your investments across multiple borrowers to mitigate potential losses.

Real Estate Investment Trusts (REITs) allow investors to invest in real estate without owning physical properties. REITs pool Money from multiple investors to buy and manage real estate assets, distributing rental income and capital gains to shareholders. This allows investors to receive help from real estate investments without the hassle of property management.

Royalties from creative works, such as books, music, and patents, can provide a steady stream of passive income. If you have a knack for writing, composing, or inventing, creating works that generate royalties can be a rewarding way to earn Money over time. Platforms like Amazon Kindle Direct Publishing and music streaming services make it easier than ever to distribute your creations to a global audience.

Crowdfunding platforms offer another unique opportunity to earn passive income. By investing in startups and small businesses through equity crowdfunding, you can receive help from their growth and Success. While this can be riskier than other forms of passive income, the potential rewards can be large if you choose suitable  projects, and selling online courses is a growing trend in the passive income world. If you have ability in a particular field, you can share your knowledge through video lessons, written content, and interactive activities. Platforms like Udemy and Teachable make reaching a broad audience easy and earning revenue from course enrollments.

Another digital product to consider is software or apps. Developing a helpful tool or app can generate ongoing revenue through sales or subscriptions. While the first development can be time-consuming and require technical skills, the potential for passive income is significant once the product is launched.

Licensing your skills or intellectual property can also create passive income streams. For example, if you have a patented invention, you can license it to companies for a fee. Similarly, if you have ability in a particular area, you can create a licensing program that allows others to use your methods or materials for a fee.

Investing in index funds and mutual funds is another way to generate passive income. These funds pool money from multiple investors to buy a diversified portfolio of stocks, bonds, or other assets. By investing in these funds, you can receive help from the overall growth of the market while earning dividends and interest.

Building a blog or YouTube channel can also lead to passive income through advertising, sponsorships, and affiliate marketing. By creating valuable content that attracts a loyal audience, you can monetize your platform in many ways. While it takes time to build an audience, the potential for passive income is large once you have a steady stream of visitors or viewers.

Investing in high-yield savings accounts or certificates of deposit (CDs) is a more conservative approach to generating passive income. While the returns may not be as high as other investments, these options provide a safe and predictable income stream. They can be an excellent choice for risk-averse investors or complement more aggressive passive income strategies.

Now that we have covered the distinct types of passive income, it is time to assess which opportunities are best suited for you. Start by considering your skills, interests, and resources. For example, if you enjoy writing and have expertise in a particular subject, creating digital products or online courses may be a good fit if you enjoy writing and have expertise in a certain specific If you have the capital to invest and are comfortable with real estate, rental properties, or REITs could be a solid choice.

It is also important to consider your risk tolerance and time commitment. Some passive income opportunities, like investing in stocks or real estate, may require a higher first investment and ongoing management. Others, like creating digital products or affiliate marketing, may require more upfront effort but can be highly achievable.

To help you decide, look at real-life examples of individuals who have successfully found and implemented passive income opportunities. Take Jane, a teacher who started creating and selling online courses in her spare time. Over a few years, she built a library of courses that now generate a sizable part of her income, allowing her to reduce her teaching hours and spend more time with her family.

Or consider Mike, an IT professional who invested in dividend-paying stocks and rental properties. By carefully investing and reinvesting earnings, he made a steady stream of passive income that supports his lifestyle and provides financial security.

These examples illustrate that passive income is achievable and can be tailored to fit your unique situation. By carefully assessing your skills, interests, and resources, you can find the best opportunities for you and start building your passive income streams.

As we continue this journey, remember that diversification is the key to Success in passive income. By spreading your investments across multiple streams, you can reduce risk and increase your chances of long-term Success. The theater chapter' on financial planning and management provides the tools you need to create a sturdy foundation for passive income ventures.

Chapter 3: Building a Strong Foundation – Financial Planning and Management

Building passive income streams requires a solid financial foundation. Even the best passive income opportunities can falter without proper  planning and management. This chapter focuses on the essential aspects of financial planning and management, ensuring you are well-prepared to embark on your passive income journey.

First, let us talk about budgeting. A well-crafted budget is the cornerstone of any successful financial plan. It helps you track your income and expenses, find areas where you can save, and distribute funds towards your passive income goals. Start by listing all your sources of income and fixed costs, such as rent or mortgage, utilities, and insurance. Then, track your variable expenses, like groceries, entertainment, and dining out. By understanding where your Money goes each month, you can make informed decisions about where to cut back and how to redirect funds toward investments.

Saving is another crucial part of financial planning. Building an emergency fund should be your priority, providing a safety net for unexpected expenses. Aim to save at least three to six months of living expenses. Once your emergency fund is in place, focus on saving passive income ventures. Automating your savings can help you stay consistent and reach your goals faster. Set up automatic transfers to a separate savings account dedicated to your passive income projects.

Investing is where the magic of passive income begins. Start by educating yourself about different investment options and their associated risks. Diversification is critical to minimizing risk and maximizing returns. Spread your investments across various asset classes, such as stocks, bonds, real estate, and digital assets. This protects your portfolio from market fluctuations and increases your chances of achieving consistent returns.

Risk management is an essential aspect of financial planning. Understand the risks associated with each passive income opportunity and take steps to mitigate them. For example, in real estate, conducting thorough market research and property inspections can help you avoid costly mistakes. In the stock market, diversifying your portfolio and investing in low-cost index funds can reduce the impact of market volatility. Always have a backup plan and be prepared to adjust your strategies as needed.

Now, let us dive into some practical fiscal management tips to support your passive income ventures. First, keep your personal and business finances separate. Open dedicated bank accounts and credit cards for your passive income projects to simplify tracking and accounting. This also makes it easier to find tax deductions and manage cash flow.

Stay organized by keeping detailed records of all your income, expenses, and investments. Use economic management software or apps to streamline this process and gain insights into your financial health. Review your financial statements regularly and adjust your budget and investment strategies to stay on track.

Tax planning is another critical aspect of fiscal management. Understanding the tax implications of your passive income streams can help you minimize your tax liability and maximize your returns. Consult with a tax professional to ensure you take advantage of all available deductions and credits. Consider setting aside a part of your passive income for tax payments to avoid surprises during tax season.

Insurance is an often-overlooked aspect of financial planning. Ensure you have adequate coverage to protect your assets and income streams. This includes health insurance, property insurance, and liability insurance. If you are investing in rental properties, consider landlord insurance to cover potential damages and loss of rental income.

Retirement planning should also be part of your overall financial strategy.  Contribute regularly to retirement accounts, such as 401(k)s or IRAs, to take advantage of tax-deferred growth. Passive income can supplement your retirement savings, providing added security and flexibility in your golden years.

Debt management is another crucial element of financial planning. High-interest debt can erode your savings and limit your ability to invest. Prioritize paying off high-interest debts, such as credit card balances and personal loans, before focusing on building passive income streams. Consider debt consolidation or refinancing options to lower interest rates and simplify payments.

Creating an estate plan is essential for protecting your assets and ensuring your financial legacy. This includes drafting a will, setting up trusts, and appointing beneficiaries for your accounts. An estate plan can help minimize taxes and legal complications for your heirs, ensuring your hard-earned wealth is passed on according to your wishes.

Building passive income streams requires a first effort that can sometimes feel overwhelming, especially when juggling existing responsibilities. However, with effective time management and strategic outsourcing, you can balance the setup phase without burning out. This chapter will provide practical tips and techniques to help you manage your time, delegate tasks, and keep a healthy work-life balance while building your passive income streams.

Chapter 4: Creating Automated Online Businesses

In today's digital age, creating automated online businesses is one of the most effective ways to generate passive income. The internet offers countless opportunities to reach a global audience, sell products and services, and earn Money with minimal ongoing effort. This chapter will guide you through the process of setting up and managing several types of online businesses that can run on autopilot.

E-commerce is a popular choice for many aspiring passive income earners. Platforms like Shopify, WooCommerce, and BigCommerce make it easy to set up an online store and start selling products. Whether you choose to sell physical goods, digital products, or dropship items, the key to Success lies in selecting the right niche and product offerings. Research market trends, find gaps in the market, and choose products with solid ability potential.

Once your store is set up, automation tools can handle many aspects of the business. For example, inventory management systems can track stock levels and automatically reorder products when needed. Customer relationship management (CRM) software can help you manage customer interactions, send automated emails, and track sales leads. Payment gateways and shipping solutions can also be integrated to streamline the checkout and delivery processes.

Affiliate marketing is another lucrative online business model. Promoting other people's products and earning a commission on sales can generate passive income without needing inventory or customer support. Start by choosing a niche that aligns with your interests and ability. Join affiliate programs through platforms like Amazon Associates, ShareASale, or CJ Affiliate, and promote products through blogs, social media, or email marketing.

Content creation is the backbone of successful affiliate marketing. Create valuable, engaging content that attracts your target audience and encourages them to click on your affiliate links. This can include product reviews, how-to guides, and informational articles. Use search engine optimization (SEO) techniques to improve your content's visibility and drive organic traffic to your site. Over time, your affiliate income can grow exponentially as your content ranks higher in search engines and gains more visibility.

Creating and selling digital products is another effective way to earn passive income online. Digital products, such as eBooks, online courses, software, and printables, can be created once and sold repeatedly with minimal ongoing effort. Platforms like Amazon Kindle Direct Publishing, Udemy, and Gumroad make distributing your digital products to a global audience easy.

When creating digital products, focus on providing value and solving problems for your audience. Conduct market research to find common pain points and develop products that address these needs. Invest time creating high-quality content and using professional design tools to enhance the presentation.

.

. Once your digital products are launched, marketing and promotion are crucial to driving sales. Leverage social media, email marketing, and online advertising to reach potential customers and generate buzz around your products.

Software and apps are another lucrative digital product category. If you have programming skills, consider developing tools or applications that solve specific problems or provide valuable functionality. Once created, software can generate ongoing revenue through sales, subscriptions, or in-app purchases. Platforms like the Apple App Store, Google Play, and software marketplaces provide distribution channels to reach a broad audience.

Membership sites and subscription services are also effective ways to generate passive income. By offering exclusive content, resources, or services to paying members, you can create a recurring revenue stream. Membership platforms like Patreon, Substack, and MemberPress make it easy to set up and manage subscription-based businesses. Focus on providing ongoing value to your members to keep subscriptions and encourage referrals.

Another promising online business model is print-on-demand. This involves creating custom designs for products like t-shirts, mugs, and posters, printed and shipped by a third-party provider only when orders are placed. Platforms like Printful, Teespring, and Redbubble handle the product and fulfillment, allowing you to focus on creating and marketing your designs. This model requires no upfront investment in inventory, making it a low-risk option for generating passive income.

Building a blog or YouTube channel can also lead to passive income through advertising, sponsorships, and affiliate marketing. Create valuable, engaging content that attracts a loyal audience, and monetize your platform in many ways. While it takes time to build an audience, the potential for passive income is large once you have a steady stream of visitors or viewers. Use SEO techniques to improve your content's visibility and drive organic traffic to your site.

One of the critical key benefits of online businesses is their scalability. Once your business is set up and automated, you can focus on scaling and growing your income streams. This can include expanding your product offerings, reaching new markets, and using fresh marketing channels. The unlimited growth potential makes online businesses a powerful tool for achieving financial independence.

In the next chapter, we will explore the world of real estate investments. You will learn how to buy, manage, and profit from rental properties and real estate through R, EITs, and crowdfunding platforms. With a solid understanding of online businesses, you will be well-equipped to diversify your passive income streams and continue building your financial future.

Chapter 5: Investing in Real Estate for Passive Income

Investing in real estate is a time-tested strategy for generating passive income. With the right approach, rental properties can provide a steady revenue stream, property value appreciation, and various tax benefits. This chapter will guide you through the process of investing in real estate, from buying properties to managing them effectively.

The first step in real estate investing is understanding the diverse types of properties available. Residential properties, such as single-family homes, duplexes, and apartment buildings, are the most common choice for individual investors. They tend to be easier to finance and manage compared to commercial properties. However, commercial properties, such as office buildings, retail spaces, and industrial facilities, can offer higher returns and longer lease terms.

Once you have decided on the property type, the type is location. Location is a critical factor in real estate success. Properties in desirable areas with good schools, low crime rates, and strong job markets tend to appreciate value and attract reliable tenants. Conduct thorough market research to find promising locations, considering facultative growth, economic stability, and infrastructure development.

Financing your real estate investment is another crucial consideration. Traditional mortgage loans are a common financing standard, but other methods include private money lenders, hard money loans, and seller financing. Each choice has its purpose, so choose the one that best fits your financial situation and essential goals. Ensure you have a good credit score and a solid financial plan to secure favorable loan terms.

Once you have secured financing, the next step is property acquisition. This involves finding suitable properties, negotiating purchase terms, and conducting due diligence. Work with a real estate agency specializing in investment properties to find the best deals. Perform thorough inspections and appraisals to ensure the property is in good condition and priced appropriately.

Managing rental properties effectively is critical to generating passive income. This includes tenant screening, property maintenance, and rent collection. Screening tenants thoroughly can prevent future problems and ensure prompt rent payments. Use credit checks, employment verification, and references to evaluate potential tenants. Once you have reliable tenants, keep the property well to satisfy them and reduce vacancy rates.

Property management can be time-consuming, especially if you own multiple properties. Consider hiring a professional property management company to handle day-to-day operations. While this comes with a cost, it can save you time and stress, allowing you to focus on other passive income ventures. Ensure the management company has a good reputation and provides comprehensive services, including tenant screening, maintenance, and financial reporting.

Real Estate Investment Trusts (REITs) offer an alternative way to invest in real estate without the hassles of property management. REITs pool Money from multiple investors to buy and manage income-producing properties. They are traded on stock exchanges, providing liquidity and diversification. By investing in REITs, you can earn a share of rental income and capital gains without owning or managing physical properties.

Crowdfunding platforms are another innovative way to invest in real estate. These platforms allow multiple investors to pool their Money to fund real estate projects, ranging from residential developments to commercial ventures. In return, investors receive a share of the property's profits. Crowdfunding can provide access to high-quality real estate deals with low minimum investments, making it accessible to a broader range of investors.

Let us explore some practical tips for maximizing your real estate investments. First, always conduct thorough market research before buying a property. Understand local market conditions, rental rates, and property values to ensure you are making a sound investment. Use tools like rental and comparative market analysis to evaluate potential properties.

Second, focus on cash flow. Positive cash flow is essential for long-term Success in real estate investing. This means your rental income should exceed your expenses, including mortgage payments, property taxes, insurance, and maintenance costs. Calculate your expected cash flow before buying a property to ensure it will generate a profit.

Third, leverage tax benefits. Real estate investors can take advantage of various tax deductions, including mortgage interest, property taxes, depreciation, and maintenance expenses. Please consult a tax professional to ensure you maximize your deductions and comply.

Fourth, build a team of professionals. Real estate investing requires ability in various areas, including finance, law, and property management. Build a network of professionals, such as real estate agents, attorneys, accountants, and contractors, to help you navigate the complexities of real estate investing.

Fifth, consider property improvements. Strategic upgrades can increase property value and rental income. Focus on improvements that provide the best return on investment, such as kitchen and bathroom remodels, energy-efficient upgrades, and curb appeal enhancements. Always balance the cost of improvements with the potential increase in rental income or property value.

Let us look at a real-world example of successful real estate investing. Meet Sarah, a teacher who started investing in rental properties to supplement her income. She began by buying a duplex in a growing neighborhood, using a combination of savings and a traditional mortgage. After making some minor renovations, she was able to rent out both units at a premium rate, generating positive cash flow each month.

Sarah reinvested her profits into more properties, gradually building a portfolio of rental properties. She hired a property management company to handle day-to-day operations, freeing up her time to focus on her teaching career and other passive income ventures. Today, Sarah enjoys a steady stream of rental income and substantial equity growth in her properties, providing financial security and flexibility.

As we move forward, remember that real estate investing is a long-term strategy. It requires patience, diligence, and ongoing effort to achieve Success. However, this approach can provide a reliable and lucrative source of passive income.

In the next chapter, we will explore investments and dividends. You will learn how to invest in dividend-paying stocks, build a diversified portfolio, and generate passive income through intelligent investment strategies. With a solid understanding of real estate, you will be well-equipped to diversify your passive income streams and continue building your financial future.

Chapter 6: Using Investments and Dividends

Investing in the stock market is another powerful way to generate passive income. By carefully selecting dividend-paying stocks and building a diversified portfolio, you can create a steady stream of income that requires minimal ongoing effort. This chapter will guide you through the basics of investing in stocks, the importance of diversification, and strategies for maximizing your returns.

First, let us understand the concept of dividend-paying stocks. Dividends are payments companies make to their shareholders, usually quarterly, as a share of the profits. When you invest in dividend-paying stocks, you receive these payments regularly, providing a reliable source of income. Companies that pay dividends tend to be financially stable and have a history of consistent earnings, making them attractive investments for income-focused investors.

To start investing in dividend-paying stocks, open a brokerage account with a reputable firm. Many online brokers offer low fees, user-friendly platforms, and educational resources to help you get started. Once your account is set up, research, and select dividend-paying stocks that align with your investment goals. Look for companies with a strong record of accomplishment of paying and increasing dividends, solid financials, and a competitive advantage in their industry.

Building a diversified portfolio is crucial to minimizing risk and maximizing returns. Diversification involves spreading your investments across various asset classes, industries, and geographies to reduce the impact of any single investment's mediocre performance. A well-diversified portfolio can weather market fluctuations and provide more stable returns.

Start by distributing your investments across different sectors, such as technology, healthcare, consumer goods, and utilities. Each industry has unique characteristics and can perform.

Differently in various economic conditions. By diversifying across sectors, you reduce the risk of your portfolio being overly affected by a downturn in any industry.

Geographic diversification is also essential. Invest in companies from different regions and countries to reduce the impact of regional economic fluctuations. International investments can provide exposure to emerging markets with high growth potential, further enhancing your portfolio's returns.

In addition to stocks, consider including other income-generating assets in your portfolio, such as bonds, real estate, and "REITs". Bonds provide regular interest payments and are less volatile than stocks, offering stability and income diversification. Real estate investments can provide rental income and property appreciation, while "REITs" offer exposure to real estate without the hassle of property management.

Let us explore some practical strategies for maximizing your returns from dividend-paying stocks. First, focus on companies with a history of consistent and growing dividends. Dividend growth is a positive indicator of a company's financial health and ability to return value to shareholders. Look for companies with a strong balance sheet, healthy cash flow, and a low payout ratio (the percentage of earnings paid as dividends).

Second, consider reinvesting your dividends. Many brokerage accounts offer dividend reinvestment plans (DRIPs) that automatically reinvest your dividend payments into added shares of the same stock. This can accelerate your portfolio's growth through compounding, as you earn dividends on your reinvested dividends over time.

Third, check your investments regularly. Stay informed about the companies in your portfolio, their financial performance, and any changes in their dividend policies. While dividend-paying stocks tend to be more stable, it is essential to stay vigilant and adjust as needed to keep a healthy portfolio.

Let us look at a real-world example of successful dividend investing. Meet John, an engineer who wanted to create a reliable source of passive income for retirement. He started by researching and selecting a diverse range of various stocks from different sectors and regions. John focused on companies with a strong history of dividend growth and solid financials.

Over the years, John reinvested his dividends through a DRIP, steadily growing his portfolio. He regularly reviewed his investments, adjusting to keep diversification and perfect returns. Today, John's portfolio generates a substantial amount of passive income, allowing him to retire comfortably and enjoy financial independence.

As we continue this journey, remember that investing in dividend-paying stocks requires patience, discipline, and ongoing effort. By building a diversified portfolio and using the power of dividends, you can create a reliable and lucrative source of passive income.

In the next chapter, we will explore the world of digital products. You will learn how to create and sell digital content, use online platforms, and generate passive income through digital product sales. With a solid understanding of investments and dividends, you can diversify your passive income streams and continue building your financial future.

Chapter 7: Creating and Selling Digital Products

The digital age has opened many opportunities for generating passive income through digital products.  Whether eBooks, online courses, software, or printables, digital products can be created once and sold repeatedly, providing a scalable and lucrative income stream. This chapter will guide you through the ping, marketing, and selling digital products effectively.

First, let us explore the types of digital products you can create. eBooks are a popular choice for writers and experts in various fields. They can cover a wide range of topics, from self-help and business to fiction and cookbooks. Online courses are another lucrative option, allowing you to share your knowledge through video lessons, written content, and interactive activities. Software and apps provide valuable tools or entertainment, while printables, such as planners, worksheets, and art prints, can cater to niche markets.

The key to Success with digital products is providing value and solving problems for your audience. Start by finding your target audience and understanding their needs and pain points. Conduct market research to decide what types of products are in demand and what gaps exist in the market. This will help you create products that resonate with your audience and stand out from the competition.

Once you have found your niche and product idea, creating your digital product is time. Focus on quality and user experience. This means writing explicit, engaging eBook content, and using professional formatting and design. Online courses should include well-produced video lessons, comprehensive written materials, and interactive elements to enhance learning. Software and apps should be user-friendly and bug-free, while printables should feature attractive designs and functional layouts.

Marketing your digital products is crucial to driving sales and generating passive income. Start by building an online presence through a website or blog. Use content marketing to attract and engage your target audience, providing valuable information about your niche. SEO techniques can help improve your website's visibility in search engines, driving organic traffic.

Social media is another powerful marketing tool. Use platforms like Facebook, Instagram, Twitter, and LinkedIn to promote your digital products, engage with your audience, and drive traffic to your website. Paid advertising on social media can also help you reach a larger audience and generate more sales.

Email marketing is an effective way to nurture leads and drive sales. Build an email list by offering a free resource or discount in exchange for visitors' email addresses. Send regular newsletters with valuable content, updates, and promotions to keep your audience engaged and encourage them to buy your digital products.

Leveraging online platforms can also help you reach a broader audience and increase sales. For eBooks, consider using Amazon Kindle Direct Publishing, which provides access to millions of readers worldwide. Online courses can be hosted on platforms like Udemy or Teachable, which offer built-in marketing tools and a large user base. Software and apps can be distributed through the Apple App Store, Google Play, and other software marketplaces.

Pricing your digital products appropriately is essential for maximizing sales and revenue. Research related products in your niche to understand pricing trends and set competitive prices. Consider offering different pricing tiers or bundles to cater to customer needs and budgets. For example, you can provide a provide provided for your product at a lower price and a premium version with added features or content at a higher price.

Customer feedback is invaluable for improving your digital products and increasing sales. Encourage your customers to leave reviews, provide feedback, and use this information to make enhancements and address any issues. Positive reviews and testimonials can also be powerful marketing tools, building trust and credibility with potential customers.

Let us look at a real-world example of successful digital product creation. Meet Emily, a graphic designer who created a series of printable planners and worksheets. She started by researching her target audience and finding a demand for beautifully designed, functional planners. Emily created high-quality printables and marketed them through her website, social media, and Etsy.

Over time, Emily built a loyal customer base and expanded her product offerings to include digital stickers and art prints. She used customer feedback to continually improve her products and increase sales. Today, Emily's digital products generate significant passive income, allowing her to focus on her design business and other creative pursuits.

As we continue this journey, remember that creating and selling digital products requires creativity, market research, and ongoing effort. By providing valuable content and effectively marketing your products, you can create a lucrative source of passive income.

In the next chapter, we will explore the world of content creation through blogs and YouTube channels. You will learn how to create engaging content, build an audience, and monetize your platform through advertising, sponsorships, and affiliate marketing. With a solid understanding of digital products, you can diversify your passive income streams and continue building your financial future.

Chapter 8: Building and Monetizing a Blog or YouTube Channel

Content creation through blogs and YouTube channels has become a popular and effective way to generate passive income. Creating valuable and engaging content can attract a loyal audience, monetize your platform, and earn Money through various revenue streams. This chapter will guide you through building and monetizing a blog or YouTube channel.

First, let us discuss the importance of choosing the right niche. Your niche should align with your interests and ability, as well as have a substantial audience demand. Conduct market research to name popular topics and gaps in the market. Whether it is cooking, travel, finance, or tech reviews, selecting a niche you are passionate about will make content creation enjoyable and sustainable.

Once you have chosen your niche, it is time to create your blog or YouTube channel. For a blog, select a user-friendly platform like WordPress or Blogger. Choose a domain name that reflects your niche and brand and invest in a professional-looking design. Create a channel name and branding for a YouTube channel that aligns with your niche. Invest in quality equipment, such as a good camera and microphone, to produce high-quality videos.

Content is king when it comes to building an audience. Focus on creating valuable, informative, engaging content that resonates with your target audience. This means authoring well-researched articles, how-to guides, and reviews for blogs. Use SEO techniques to improve your content for search engines and drive organic traffic to your site. For YouTube, create visually appealing and well-edited videos that provide value and entertainment. Consistency is vital, so set up a regular posting schedule to keep your audience engaged and coming back for more.

Building an audience takes time and effort. Promote your content through social media, email marketing, and online communities related to your niche. Engage with your audience by responding to comments, taking part in discussions, and asking for feedback. Building a loyal community around your blog or YouTube channel is crucial for long-term Success.

Monetizing your blog or YouTube channel involves several revenue streams. Advertising is a standard method that means Money is paid to advertise on your platform. For blogs, join ad networks like "Google AdSense" to display relevant ads on your site. For YouTube, enable monetization through the YouTube Partner Program to earn Money from ads shown on your videos.

Affiliate marketing is another effective monetization strategy. Promote products or services related to your niche and earn a commission on sales through your affiliate links. Write product reviews, create how-to guides,

and include affiliate links in your content. For YouTube, include affiliate links in your video descriptions and mention them in your videos.

Sponsorships can provide a significant source of income for established bloggers and YouTubers. Companies will pay you to promote their products or services to your audience. Reach out to brands related to your niche and propose collaboration opportunities. Create sponsored content that aligns with your audience's interests and keeps your city.

Selling digital products is another way to monetize your platform. Create eBooks, online courses, printables, or software that provide value to your audience. Promote these products through your blog or YouTube channel and use your existing audience to drive sales. This can provide a reliable and scalable source of passive income.

Merchandising can also be a lucrative choice. Create branded merchandise, such as t-shirts, mugs, and stickers, and sell them to your audience. Use print-on-demand services like Printful or Teespring to handle production and fulfillment, allowing you to focus on design and marketing.

Let us look at a real-world example of successful content creation and monetization. Meet Alex, a tech enthusiast who started a YouTube channel reviewing the latest gadgets. He focused on creating high-quality, informative videos that provided value to his audience. Over time, Alex built a loyal following and began monetizing his channel through ads, affiliate marketing, and sponsorships.

Alex expanded his content to include how-to guides and tech news, further engaging his audience. He also created an eBook on smartphone photography, which became a bestseller among his followers. Today, Alex's YouTube channel generates substantial passive income, allowing him to pursue his passion full-time.

As we continue this journey, remember that building and monetizing a blog or YouTube channel requires creativity, consistency, and ongoing effort. By providing valuable content and effectively monetizing your platform, you can create a scalable and lucrative source of passive income.

In the next section, chapter, you will balance initial efforts with current responsibilities. During the first setup phase, you will learn time management techniques, outsourcing strategies, and practical tips for keeping balance and  avoiding burnout. With a solid understanding of content creation, you will be well-equipped to diversify your passive income streams and continue building your financial future.

Chapter 9: Balancing Initial Effort with Current Responsibilities

Building passive income streams requires a first effort that sometimes feels overwhelming, especially when juggling existing responsibilities.

However, with effective time management and strategic outsourcing, you can balance the setup phase without burning out with effective time management and strategic outsourcing. This chapter will provide practical tips and techniques to help you manage your time, delegate tasks, and keep a healthy work-life balance while building passive income streams.

First, let us balance effective time management between your passive income projects and your current responsibilities. Start by finding your most productive hours of the day and distributing that time to work on your passive income ventures. Use calendars, to-do lists, and productivity apps to organize your tasks and stay on track.

Prioritization is critical to many crucial multiple responsibilities. Break down your projects into smaller, manageable tasks and prioritize them based on importance and deadlines. Focus on high-impact tasks that move you closer to your goals. Use techniques like the Eisenhower Matrix to categorize tasks into urgent, meaningful, and less critical, allowing you to focus on what matters most.

Time blocking is another effective technique. Allocate specific blocks of time for different tasks and stick to your schedule. This helps prevent multitasking and ensures you dedicate focused time to each responsibility. For example, set aside time in the morning for your primary job, afternoons for passive income projects, and evenings for personal and family time.

Delegating tasks can save you time and reduce stress. Name tasks that can be outsourced or delegated to others, such as administrative work, content creation, or customer support. Platforms like Upwork, Fiverr, and TaskRabbit provide access to freelancers and virtual assistants who can handle various tasks, allowing you to focus on high-priority activities.

Outsourcing is particularly beneficial for income projects that require specialized skills or momentous time investment. For example, if you are creating an online course, you can hire a video editor to produce professional-quality videos or a graphic designer to make course materials. This saves time and ensures your products are of high quality.

Automation tools can streamline repetitive tasks and free up your time. Use email marketing automation to send scheduled newsletters and promotional emails. Social media scheduling tools like Hootsuite and Buffer can manage your social media posts, ensuring consistent engagement without constant manual effort. E-commerce platforms offer automation features for inventory management, order processing, and customer support.

Setting realistic goals is crucial for keeping balance. Break down your long-term goals into short-term milestones and celebrate your progress. This helps you stay motivated and focused without feeling overwhelmed. Remember that building passive income streams is a marathon, not a sprint. It is important to pace yourself and avoid burnout.

Maintaining a healthy work-life balance is essential for long-term Success. Allocate time for self-care, exercise, and leisure activities to recharge and prevent burnout. Set boundaries between work and personal time and communicate these boundaries with family and friends. Taking regular breaks and disconnecting from work can improve productivity and overall well-being.

Let us look at a real-world example of effective time management and delegation. Meet Lisa, a marketing manager who wanted to create passive income through a blog and online courses. She started by finding her most productive hours and dedicating that time to her projects. Lisa used time blocking to balance her job, passive income ventures, and personal time.

To save time, Lisa outsourced tasks like website design, video editing, and social media management to freelancers. She also used automation tools to schedule blog posts and email newsletters. By delegating and automating tasks, Lisa was able to formulate high-quality content and engage with her audience. Today, Lisa successfully manages her marketing career and passive income projects without feeling overwhelmed.

As we continue this journey, remember that balancing initial effort with current responsibilities requires effective time management, delegation, and self-care. Implementing these strategies allows you to build your passive income streams without sacrificing your well-being.

 The next chapter will conclude our journey by embracing the auto-pilot hustle lifestyle. You will learn how to support and grow your passive income streams, stay committed to your long-term vision, and enjoy the benefits of financial independence. You can continue building your financial future with a solid understanding of balancing effort and responsibilities.

Chapter 10: Conclusion – Embracing the Auto-Pilot Hustle Lifestyle

It is time to fully embrace the auto-pilot hustle lifestyle. This chapter will summarize the key lessons learned,  provide strategies for keeping and growing your passive income streams, and inspire you to stay committed to your long-term vision of financial independence and a relaxed lifestyle.

First, let us recap the main points discussed in this book. We have explored various passive income opportunities, from real estate and investments to digital products and online businesses. Each type of passive income requires a first effort and ongoing management, but with the right approach, they can provide a reliable and scalable source of income. We have also covered essential financial planning and management strategies, time management techniques, and practical tips for balancing initial effort with current responsibilities.

Maintaining your passive income streams requires regular monitoring and adjustment. Track your investments, business performance, and market trends to ensure your income streams still are profitable. Be prepared to make changes as needed, whether diversifying your portfolio, updating your digital products, or exploring new passive income opportunities. Staying informed and adaptable is critical to long-term Success.

Growing your passive income streams involves reinvesting your earnings and continuously seeking new opportunities. Reinvesting dividends, rental income, or profits from digital products can accelerate your portfolio's growth and increase your overall returns. Look for ways to expand your existing income streams, such as adding new products, reaching new markets, or using fresh marketing channels.

Staying committed to your long-term vision is crucial for achieving financial independence. Set clear, achievable goals and regularly review your progress. Stay motivated by celebrating your milestones and reminding yourself of the benefits of a passive income lifestyle. Whether it is more time for family, pursuing passions, or achieving financial security, keep your ultimate goals in mind.

Enjoying the benefits of the auto-pilot hustle lifestyle means more than just financial independence. It is about having the freedom to spend your time as you choose, pursuing activities that bring you joy and fulfillment. Embrace the flexibility and opportunities that come with passive income and use them to create a life that aligns with your values and aspirations.

As we conclude this book, remember that building passive income streams is a journey, not a destination. It requires ongoing effort, learning, and  adaptation. But with the right mindset and strategies, you can achieve financial independence and enjoy a more relaxed and fulfilling lifestyle.

Let us look at a final inspirational story. Meet David, a software engineer who started building passive income streams through real estate, dividend stocks, and an online business. Over the years, David diligently invested his earnings, diversified his portfolio, and continuously sought new opportunities. Today, David enjoys financial independence, traveling the world with his family, and pursuing his passion for photography. His passive income streams provide the security and flexibility he has always dreamed of.

David's story illustrates that the auto-pilot hustle lifestyle is achievable with dedication, thoughtful planning, and a willingness to learn and adapt. It is about creating a life where financial security and personal freedom go hand in hand.

As we conclude, let us leave you with a memorable quote: "Success is not the key to happiness. Happiness is the key to Success. If you love what you are doing, you will be successful." Embrace the journey, enjoy the process, and use the principles discussed in this book to create a life you love.

Thank you for joining us on this journey. We hope this book has offered valuable insights, practical strategies, and the inspiration to pursue your passive income goals. Remember, the path to financial independence and a relaxed lifestyle is within your reach. Start today, stay committed, and enjoy the rewards of the auto-pilot hustle lifestyle.

Chapter 11: Nurturing a Growth Mindset for Sustained Success

As we delve into the final chapters of our journey, we see that having an  efficient mindset is the key to sustained Success. The essential concept of a growth mindset is critical for anyone looking to build and support passive income streams. A growth mindset is the belief that abilities and intelligence can be developed through dedication, hard work, and continuous learning. This chapter will explore nurturing a growth mindset, overcoming obstacles, and continuously improving your passive income ventures.

A growth mindset starts with self-awareness. Understand your strengths and weaknesses and be open to feedback and innovative ideas. Self-awareness allows you to name areas for improvement and recognize growth opportunities. It also helps you stay motivated and focused on your long-term goals.

Embrace challenges as opportunities to learn and grow. Instead of viewing obstacles as setbacks, see them as valuable learning experiences. Every challenge you meet in your passive income journey is a chance to develop new skills, gain insights, and become more resilient. This positive outlook will help you stay persistent and overcome difficulties.

Set realistic and achievable goals to keep a sense of progress and accomplishment. Break down your long-term aims into smaller, manageable milestones. This approach makes your goals more attainable and provides a clear roadmap for your journey. Celebrate your achievements along the way to stay motivated and build momentum.

Continuous learning is a critical part of a growth mindset. Stay curious and open to current information, trends, and strategies. Invest time educating yourself about passive income opportunities, monetary management techniques, and market developments. Read books, attend seminars, take online courses, and engage with communities related to your interests.

Surround yourself with a supportive network. Connect with like-minded individuals who share your goals and aspirations. Join online forums, social media groups, or local meetups focused on passive income and financial independence. A supportive network provides encouragement, accountability, and valuable insights from others who have walked the same path.

Failure is an inevitable part of any journey, but it is also a powerful teacher. Learn to view failure as a steppingstone to success. Analyze your mistakes, find what went wrong, and use that knowledge to improve your strategies. Remember that every successful person has experienced setbacks, and it is their ability to learn from those experiences that sets them apart.

Maintain a positive attitude and focus on the possibilities rather than the limitations. A positive mindset attracts opportunities and helps you stay resilient in the face of challenges. Practice gratitude by regularly reflecting on your accomplishments and progress. This habit fosters a sense of fulfillment and keeps you motivated to continue your journey.

Take calculated risks and step out of your comfort zone. Growth requires pushing beyond your current limits and trying new things. Evaluate the potential risks and rewards of different opportunities and make informed decisions. Even if a venture fails, the experience and knowledge gained will be invaluable for future endeavors.

Developing discipline and consistency is crucial for long-term Success. Building passive income streams often requires sustained effort and patience. Establish a routine that includes regular work on your passive income projects and stick to it. Consistency builds habits, and habits lead to progress and results.

Adaptability is another essential trait of a growth mindset. The world of passive income is dynamic and ever-changing. Stay flexible and be willing to adjust your strategies as needed. Keep an eye on market trends, technological advancements, and changes in consumer behavior. Adapting to new circumstances ensures you stay relevant and continue to thrive.

Mindfulness and self-care play a significant role in nurturing a growth mindset. Take time to relax, reflect, and recharge. Practicing mindfulness helps you stay present and focused, reducing stress and enhancing your overall well-being. Incorporate meditation, exercise, and hobbies into your routine to keep a healthy balance.

Seek out mentors and role models who can provide guidance and inspiration. Learning from those who have already achieved Success can shorten your learning curve and help you avoid common pitfalls. Do not hesitate to reach out to experienced individuals for advice and support.

Document your journey and track your progress. Keeping a journal or detailed records of your activities, successes, and challenges can offer valuable insights. Revi's journey helps you recognize patterns, make informed decisions, and celebrate growth.

Practice resilience and persistence. The journey to building passive income streams is rarely linear. There will be difficulties, and it is essential to stay coming. Resilience allows you to bounce back from setbacks, while persistence ensures you keep moving forward despite obstacles.

As we wrap up this chapter, remember that nurturing a growth mindset is ongoing. It requires continuous effort, self-reflection, and a willingness to learn and adapt. By embracing a growth mindset, you will be better equipped to navigate the challenges of building passive income streams and achieve long-term Success.

In the concluding chapter, we will discuss the importance of giving back and making a positive impact to use your Success to benefit others, create a legacy, and contribute to a better world. With a solid understanding of the growth mindset, you will be well-prepared to not achieve financial independence and make a meaningful difference in the lives of others.

Chapter 12: Giving Back and Creating a Legacy

As we move forward, it is important to reevaluate the broader impact of achieving financial independence through passive income. Building and keeping multiple income streams not only provides personal freedom and  security but also offers the opportunity to give back and create a legacy. This chapter will explore how to use your Success to make a positive difference in the world, support causes you care about, and leave a meaningful legacy for future generations.

Giving back starts with identifying causes that resonate with you. Consider the issues and communities that matter most to you, whether it is education, healthcare, environmental conservation, or social justice. Your firsthand experiences, values, and passions can guide you in selecting the causes you want to support. Aligning your efforts with your values will help you find greater fulfillment and motivation in your philanthropic activity.

Financial contributions are a powerful way to support your chosen causes. Donating some of your passive income to charities, non-profits, or community organizations can significantly affect you. Research the organizations you wish to support to ensure they align with your values and use donations effectively. Consider setting up recurring contributions to provide consistent support over time.

Volunteering your time and skills is another impactful way to give back. Many organizations rely on volunteers to support their missions and operations. Whether you have ability in marketing, finance, education, or another field, your skills can be valuable to non-profits and community groups. Volunteering helps others and enriches your life with new experiences and connections.

Creating educational resources and sharing your knowledge can also make a positive impact. Consider mentoring aspiring entrepreneurs, offering workshops, or creating content that educates others about passive income and financial independence. You can inspire and empower others to achieve their financial goals by sharing your journey and insights.

Supporting local businesses and communities can profoundly affect your area's economic well-being in local enterprises, shop at small businesses, and take part in community events. Your support helps create jobs, stimulate local economies, and build a sense of community. Additionally, consider joining local business organizations or chambers of commerce to network and collaborate with local entrepreneurs.

Establishing a charitable foundation or trust is another way to create a lasting impact. These entities support the causes you care about, ensuring your philanthropic efforts continue for generations. Work with legal and financial advisors to set up an establishment or trust that aligns with your goals and values.

Advocacy and raising awareness are crucial components of giving back. Use your platform and influence to advocate for the issues that matter to you. Whether through social media, public speaking, or writing, raising awareness can mobilize others to act and support your chosen causes. Advocacy efforts can lead to meaningful local, national, or even global change.

Creating a legacy involves more than just financial contributions; it is about leaving a lasting positive impact on the world. Document your values, experience, and s, and for o pas for future generations. Write a memoir, create videos, or prove a family mission statement that outlines your commitment to making a difference. These actions ensure that your legacy of giving back and creating positive change continues beyond your lifetime.

Let us look at a real-world example of creating a legacy. Meet Michael, an entrepreneur who built multiple passive  income streams through real estate and online businesses. After achieving financial independence, Michael decided to focus on giving back. He set up a charitable foundation that supports education and mentorship programs for underprivileged youth. Michael also volunteers as a mentor, sharing his knowledge and experiences with young entrepreneurs.

Through his foundation, Michael has funded scholarships, built educational facilities, and supported various community initiatives through his foundation. His advice through his advocacy efforts has raised awareness about the importance of education and entrepreneurship, inspiring others to get involved. Michael's legacy of giving back has created a ripple effect, positively affecting countless lives and communities.

As we conclude this book, remember that the journey to financial independence through passive independence is about more than personal Success. It is an opportunity to positively impact, to support cases you care about, and leave a meaningful legacy. By using your Success to give back and create change, you contribute to a better world for future generations.

Nap-time Net-worth Neutron Cash Cushion Climax Conclusion

As we draw this incredible journey to a close, it is time to reflect on the  transformative power of the auto-pilot hustle lifestyle. You have explored the myriad ways to create passive income, learned to build a solid financial foundation, and discovered how to balance effort with relaxation. Now, let us wrap up this book with an explosive conclusion that summarizes our journey and propels you into action with renewed vigor and enthusiasm.

First, let us recap the fundamental principles that have guided us throughout this book. Passive income is the key to financial freedom, offering the promise of earning Money with minimal ongoing effort. It is about working smarter, not harder, and using your time and resources to build income streams that continue to flow even when you are not actively working. This lifestyle is not a fantasy but a reality that many have achieved, and now, with the knowledge and strategies you have gained, you can too.

The allure of passive income lies in its ability to provide financial security and the freedom to design your life as you see fit. No longer bound by the constraints of a 9-to-5 job, you can pursue passions, spend time with loved ones, and wake up each day knowing your financial future is secure. The journey to this point requires dedication, smart planning, and a willingness to learn and adapt. But the rewards, as you have seen through the many examples and case studies, are well worth the effort.

One of the most crucial lessons we have emphasized is the importance of diversification. By spreading your investments and income streams across various sources, you reduce risk and increase your chances of sustained Success. Whether it is through real estate, investments, digital products, or online businesses, having multiple streams of passive income ensures you are not reliant on a sole source, providing stability and resilience.

Building a strong financial foundation is essential for supporting your passive income ventures. From budgeting and saving to investing and risk management, we have covered the key aspects of financial planning. These principles are the bedrock upon which your passive income streams are built, ensuring you have the resources and stability to pursue your goals without financial stress.

Automation and delegation are your allies in the auto-pilot hustle. By using technology and outsourcing tasks, you can reduce your workload and focus on strategic growth. The examples of automated online businesses, from e-commerce to affiliate marketing, highlight the power of systems and processes in generating income on autopilot. These strategies allow you to step back and enjoy the fruits of your labor without being constantly tied to your work.

The importance of a growth mindset cannot be overstated. Embracing challenges, learning from failures, and continuously seeking improvement are hallmarks of successful individuals. The stories of those who have achieved financial independence through passive income illustrate that setbacks are part of the journey, but resilience and persistence pave the way to Success. A growth mindset keeps you motivated and adaptable, ready to seize new opportunities and overcome obstacles.

As you move forward, remember that time management is key to balancing your passive income projects with existing responsibilities. Effective prioritization, time blocking, and the use of productivity tools help you stay organized and focused. By delegating and automating tasks, you free up time for what truly matters, whether it is strategic planning, personal growth, or simply enjoying life.

Creating and supporting passive income streams is a marathon, not a sprint. It requires patience, discipline, and a long-term perspective. The first effort you invest in setting up your income streams will pay off in the form of sustained financial freedom and flexibility. Stay committed to your goals, and do not be discouraged by setbacks. Each step you take brings you closer to the lifestyle you want.

In the grand scheme of things, financial independence is just the beginning. The true value of the auto-pilot hustle lifestyle lies in the freedom it affords you. Freedom to pursue passions, spend time with loved ones, travel the world, or simply relax and enjoy the present moment. It is about living life on your terms, unencumbered by financial stress or the demands of a traditional job.

As you reflect on the journey we have taken together, think about the possibilities that now lie ahead. The knowledge and strategies you have gained empower you to take control of your financial future and create a life that aligns with your values and desires. The auto-pilot hustle is not just a means to an end but a way of living that prioritizes balance, fulfillment, and freedom.

To leave you with an inspiring story, consider Sarah, a single mother who transformed her life through the principles of the auto-pilot hustle. Struggling to balance work and family, Sarah began exploring passive income opportunities. She started with a small blog, sharing her journey of financial independence. As her blog gained traction, she diversified into affiliate marketing, digital products, and eventually, real estate investments.

Today, Sarah's steady stream of passive income allows her to spend quality time with her children, travel, and pursue her passions. Her journey was not without challenges, but her  resilience and dedication paid off. Sarah's story is a testament to the transformative power of the auto-pilot hustle lifestyle and a reminder that anyone can achieve financial freedom with the right mindset and strategies.

We leave you with a call to action as we conclude this book. Apply the principles and strategies you have learned to your own life. Start small, stay consistent, and keep your long-term goals in sight. The journey to financial independence and a leisurely lifestyle is within your reach. Embrace the auto-pilot hustle, and let it guide you to a future filled with freedom, fulfillment, and endless possibilities.

Thank you for joining us on this journey. We hope this book has provided you with valuable insights, practical  strategies, and the inspiration to pursue your passive income goals. Remember, the path to financial independence is within your reach, and the opportunities to create a life you love are endless. Start today, stay committed, and enjoy the rewards of the auto-pilot hustle lifestyle. Here is to a future where you stay in bed, make Money, and get up only when you feel like it!

This concludes the book:
"How to Stay in Bed, Make Money, then Get Up Only When You Feel Like It: The Auto Pilot Hustle Book"

Check Out A Book Bundle From
Brian's Other Famous Titles
"How To Get Past The Gatekeepers and
Get To Your Goal In Life:
A Personal Guide to Being Persistent"

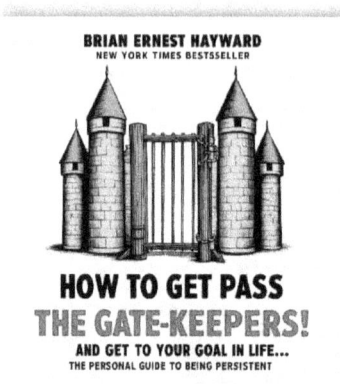

Bibliography

1. **Covey, Stephen R.** *The 7 Habits of Highly Effective People: Powerful Lessons in Personal Change*. Simon & Schuster, 1989.

2. **Hill, Napoleon.** *Think and Grow Rich*. The Ralston Society, 1937.

3. **Kiyosaki, Robert T.** *Rich Dad Poor Dad: What the Rich Teach Their Kids About Money That the Poor and Middle Class Do Not!*. Plata Publishing, 1997.

4. **Tracy, Brian.** *Goals!: How to Get Everything You Want Faster Than You Ever Thought Possible*. Berrett-Koehler Publishers, 2003.

5. **Sinek, Simon.** *Start with Why: How Great Leaders Inspire Everyone to Take Action*. Portfolio, 2009.

6. **Dweck, Carol S.** *Mindset: The New Psychology of Success*. Ballantine Books, 2006.

7. **Vaynerchuk, Gary.** *Crush It!: Why NOW Is the Time to Cash In on Your Passion*. HarperStudio, 2009.

8. **Cardone, Grant.** *The 10X Rule: The Only Difference Between Success and Failure*. Wiley, 2011.

9. **Ferriss, Timothy.** *The 4-Hour Workweek: Escape 9-5, Live Anywhere, and Join the New Rich*. Crown Publishing Group, 2007.

10. **Thiel, Peter.** *Zero to One: Notes on Startups, or How to Build the Future*. Crown Business, 2014.

11. **Collins, Jim.** *Good to Great: Why Some Companies Make the Leap... and Others Don't*. HarperBusiness, 2001.

12. **Schultz, Howard, and Joanne Gordon.** *Onward: How Starbucks Fought for Its Life without Losing Its Soul*. Rodale Books, 2011.

13. **Maxwell, John C.** *The 21 Irrefutable Laws of Leadership: Follow Them and People Will Follow You*. Thomas Nelson, 1998.

14. **Sincero, Jen.** *You Are a Badass at Making Money: Master the Mindset of Wealth*. Viking, 2017.

15. **Dalio, Ray.** *Principles: Life and Work*. Simon & Schuster, 2017.

NOTES

www.ingramcontent.com/pod-product-compliance
Lightning Source LLC
Chambersburg PA
CBHW071929210526
45479CB00002B/612